The Last
American Rainforest

TONGASS

by SHELLEY GILL

illustrated by SHANNON CARTWRIGHT

The Last American Rainforest
TONGASS

**Printed on TREE-FREE
paper in the U.S.A.**

Sincere thanks to all those hardy folks who took time to read and
respond to the text of Tongass: K.J. Metcalf, Susan Rogers, Gretchen
Legler, Michelle Kaelke, Dan Ketchum and Fred Harnisch and my bud joe.

Author's note

To write about the Tongass is to write about one of the last
best places left on the planet. This is primarily a story about a
forest…but to exclude the people of the area would leave only
half the story told. The Tlingit, Haida and Tsimshian cultures
spring from the soul of the rainforest. It is with great respect
and honor that we refer to their culture and their cultural symbols.

The Last American Rainforest

To the people of Southeast Alaska, this place is called simply, the Tongass. The name comes from a clan of Tlingit Indians who once lived on an island near Ketchikan, Alaska. Tongass National Forest lies in the heart of one of the world's largest temperate rainforests. Consisting primarily of spruce, cedar and hemlock, the forest wriggles north from British Columbia's Queen Charlotte Islands through Southeast Alaska to Kodiak Island. The national forest is located in a region known as the Alexander Archipelago.

Life in the Tongass depends on water; water that oozes black and boggy from glacial silt; water that trickles a melody down round-edged rock. It is a land smothered in fog and drizzle. Think of the sideways rain during the first winter storm. Hear the smashing tempest that rips down the mountain in the spring. Everywhere you hear the music of water. It begins with a fine, misty rain. The glacial and snowfield melt, the rivers and streams, the lakes, the slanting rain (200 inches a year) and the enveloping mists all provide a constant movement of water. Rain blown in from the sea bathes the glaciers and alpine high country, the forests of yellow cedar and Sitka spruce, the low country — the tidewater marshes, muskeg and bogs. Moisture promotes decay which nurtures the forest and streams.

Spotted frog

TONGASS

Two hundred years ago, Tongass lay untouched — just a piece of a vast land of forests that stretched from Maine to Michigan, from Florida to New York, California and Oregon to Washington, Canada to Alaska. The old growth redwood, sequoias and firs, the towering white pine of Michigan and Minnesota, the cypress of Florida are all silent voices now. But the Tongass remains. Undisturbed for the last 5000 years, it features one of the rarest ecosystems on earth. Some of the ancient old growth trees here are more than 800 years old. Tongass is home to the largest populations of brown bears, bald eagles and salmon on the planet.

Over time plants and animals have adapted to the cool, misty mountains, the glaciers and fiords. They have become a vast interrelated family, from the high canopy where murrelets nest to the understory where deer and lynx find food. Both marine and land animals depend on the mountains, the sea and the forest to survive. Life in the Tongass is woven together like the strands of root in a Tlingit spruce root hat. Clear water, thick with spawning salmon, you are the warp. Brown bear, eagle and deer are the weft. Root woven over root, one strand atop another, each strand depending on the next, round and round until the hat is whole, strong and complete.

Rough-skinned newt

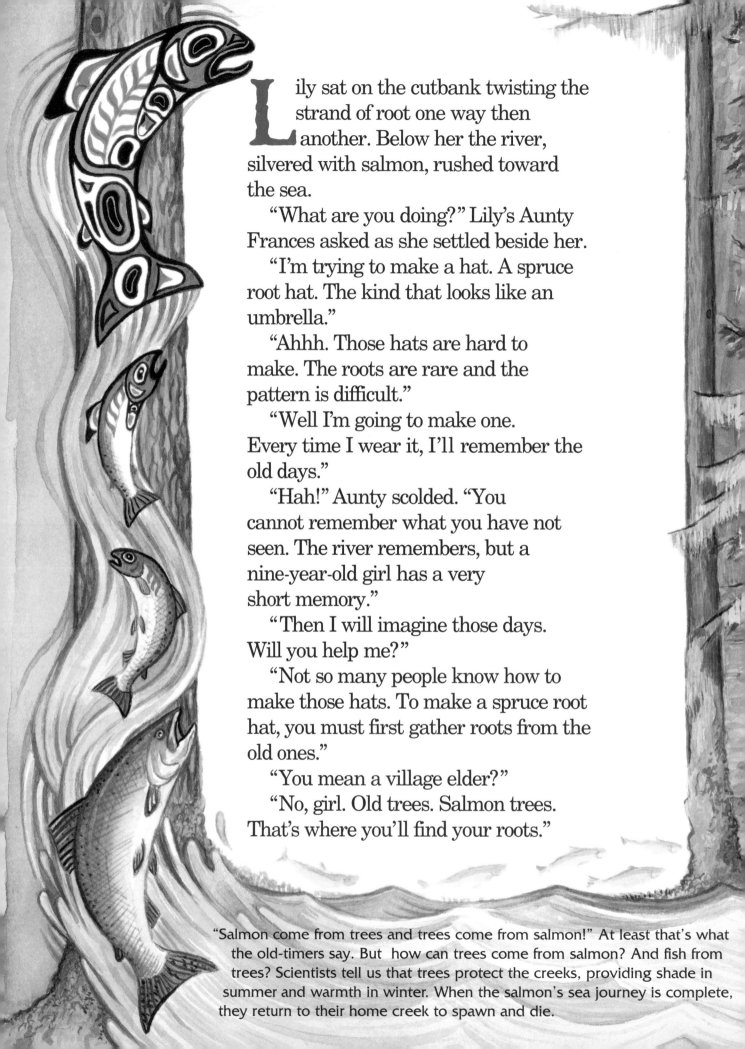

Lily sat on the cutbank twisting the strand of root one way then another. Below her the river, silvered with salmon, rushed toward the sea.

"What are you doing?" Lily's Aunty Frances asked as she settled beside her.

"I'm trying to make a hat. A spruce root hat. The kind that looks like an umbrella."

"Ahhh. Those hats are hard to make. The roots are rare and the pattern is difficult."

"Well I'm going to make one. Every time I wear it, I'll remember the old days."

"Hah!" Aunty scolded. "You cannot remember what you have not seen. The river remembers, but a nine-year-old girl has a very short memory."

"Then I will imagine those days. Will you help me?"

"Not so many people know how to make those hats. To make a spruce root hat, you must first gather roots from the old ones."

"You mean a village elder?"

"No, girl. Old trees. Salmon trees. That's where you'll find your roots."

"Salmon come from trees and trees come from salmon!" At least that's what the old-timers say. But how can trees come from salmon? And fish from trees? Scientists tell us that trees protect the creeks, providing shade in summer and warmth in winter. When the salmon's sea journey is complete, they return to their home creek to spawn and die.

Their bodies decay and the nutrients feed new generations of just-hatched salmon struggling in the first weeks of life to survive. These salmon swim downstream; the trees grow taller and the circle begins again. Old-timers call the big trees along a creek 'salmon trees.'

Mussel shells were used to split the root

Early next morning
Lily and Aunty Frances hiked
up the mountain trail. They were
searching for a special tree
called a shay-kee. The hundred-year-old
spruce had the long, thin roots they
needed to weave a hat. As she walked,
Frances used her stout digging stick
to push the spiny devil's club
and alder aside.

Digging roots

Women used digging sticks to prod for roots. When they found one, they followed it to the end, lifting and digging carefully. The roots were rolled in loose coils. Before the sap dried, the coils were steamed under a layer of mud covered with hot coals. The women stripped the bark off by drawing the slightly roasted root through a split stick called an eena (ee-nah.) The coils were stored for the summer in flat boxes to cure until the weavers had time in the winter to make their baskets and hats. Once cured, the weaver split the root by holding it in her front teeth and sliding her thumb and fingernail along its middle. Spruce roots were used to weave hats, baskets, fish traps, bags and mats.

Stripping bark with the eena

They scrambled over huge snags following a bear trail edged with dwarf dogwood. In the misty shadows of big spruce and hemlock, a thick ground cover of needles swallowed all sound.

Lily threw back her head and let her eyes wander up one of the giant tapered columns of blue and brown. It was high noon yet only the tops of the trees were kissed with light.

In the hush Lily heard the whisking wings of a big blue dragonfly as it darted through the buckbean. Ahead, spears of sunlight cut shafts in the forest roof.

In winter the Taku winds tore trees from their roots. When one fell it took others with it. Now, in the clearing, berries and brambles searched for the warmth of the rare light.

Nursery trees are the hulks of old growth trees that fall and rot. They provide a home to a variety of insects, animals and birds as well as a place for spruce, cedar and hemlock seedlings. The downed tree decomposes, feeding nutrients back into the soil. Just after a rain, if you stand back and look, the trees appear to steam.

When the humidity is high, the trees actually exhale vapor and a cloud begins to form. This has often mystified man. Perhaps the notion of living, breathing trees makes some humans feel uneasy. Perhaps when pondering these giants we are reminded of how young humanity is while the history of these trees stretches back to the Crusades, when they were seedlings in an already ancient forest.

Frances and Lily stood quietly, letting the beauty of the land wash over them. From their mountain north the white peaks of the Coastal Range cut a ragged outline against a lavender sky.

A huge grinding river of ice hung between the mountains, dipping its jagged edge in the frigid water of the sound. The sea seemed shot with silver; a liquid mirror of flashing metal.

Harbor Porpoise

Killer Whale

Gray Whale

Humpback Whale

Kittlitz's Murrelet

Rhinoceros Auklet

Tufted Puffin

Horned Puffin

Least Sandpipers

Greater Yellowlegs

Semipalmated Plovers

Harlequin Duck

Common Goldeneye

Surfscoter

Canada Goose

Once 3,000-foot deep rivers of ice covered this place. The glaciers cut U-shaped valleys from the heart of the mountains. When the glaciers melted they left gravel and silt behind. Because gravel drains quickly, only hardy, deep-rooted plants like dwarf fireweed and lupine grow. Where the ice melted and left silt the water stagnated and muskeg and blackwater ponds developed.

"The people of the Northwest Coast have always had their back to the forest and their face to the sea," Frances told Lily.

"In the old days we came to the forest for cedar to carve totems and canoes. The trees gave us boxes to store food, paddles, tools and the masks of our shamans. These trees have sheltered and fed our people for thousands of years."

Frances gave Lily a sharp look.

"This forest is like your spruce root hat. From the smallest plant to the eight-hundred-year-old spruce, each fiber, each living thing, depends on the next to survive. Foul the stream and the brown bear starves. Break the weave and the forest will wither."

The Northwest Coast people of Alaska are the Tlingit, the Tsimshian and the Haida. They believed a spirit, Yake, lives in all things. Surrounding themselves with beauty in the objects they made — baskets, hats and carvings — they respected both trees and animals.

Felling a tree by burning and adzing

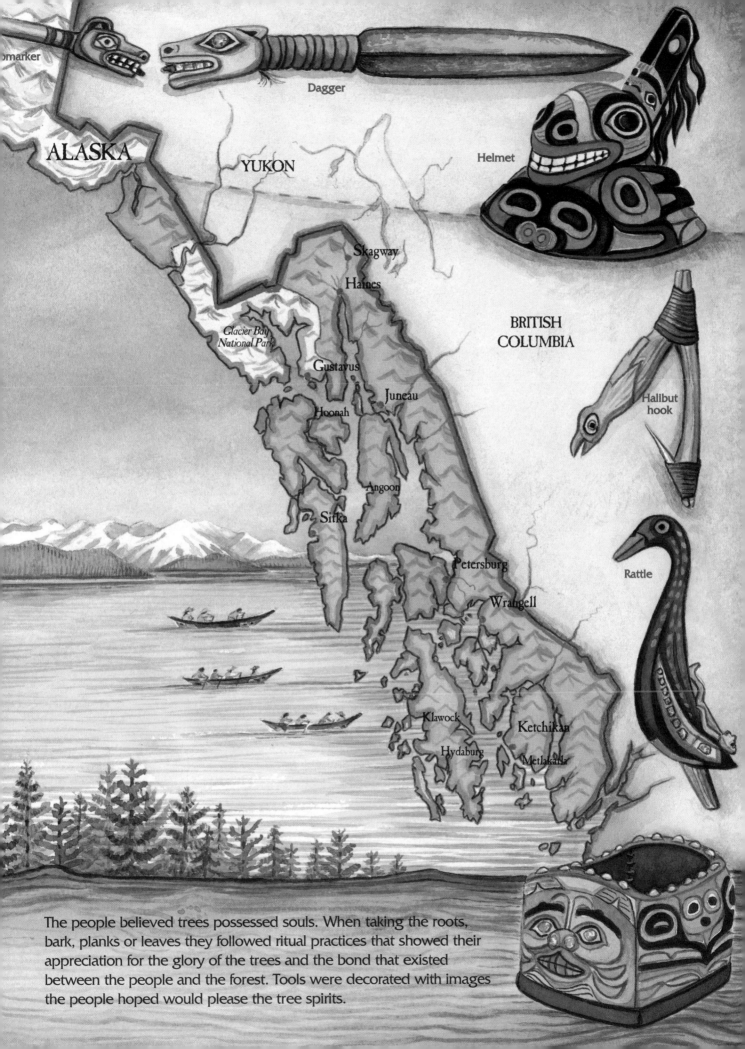

ALASKA

YUKON

BRITISH COLUMBIA

Glacier Bay National Park

Skagway

Haines

Gustavus

Hoonah

Juneau

Angoon

Sitka

Petersburg

Wrangell

Klawock

Hydaburg

Ketchikan

Metlakatla

marker

Dagger

Helmet

Halibut hook

Rattle

The people believed trees possessed souls. When taking the roots, bark, planks or leaves they followed ritual practices that showed their appreciation for the glory of the trees and the bond that existed between the people and the forest. Tools were decorated with images the people hoped would please the tree spirits.

Octopus

Butter clams

King crab

Dungeness crab

Shri

Suddenly a great whoosh of
sound exploded from the sea.
A fountain of spray fell across the
water's surface as the broad back
of a humpback whale rose, glistening,
sliding in an arc, foot by foot by foot,
until the gigantic black flukes flipped
forward and disappeared with barely
a ripple.

Frances sighed.

"The rivers were choked with fish
then. Orcas had easy hunting. So did the
seals and sea lions. Our lives were easy.
They depended on the tides, the seasons,
the land. But change has come. Now the
salmon are fewer, the herring nearly gone.
We once lived with the land as partners.
Now we take and take. Not just the Indian,
but all people. We all take too much."

Horse clam

Cockles

Dulce

Urchins

Limpets

Halibut

Herring

Salmon

Sea lettuce

Bull kelp

Mussels

The sea holds the riches that have filled Indian baskets for centuries:
mussels, clams, salmon, herring, halibut, cod and a dozen different kinds
of crab, limpets, seaweed and the delicate herring eggs that cling to the kelp.
There is an old saying that describes the importance of the sea to the people
of the Northwest Coast — "When the tide is out, the table is set!"

Lily's eyes were drawn to the mountainside above her village. Once a blanket of green, now an ugly gash of gray stumps and slash stretched from sky to sea.

"Yup," Frances grunted. "People are clever. But sometimes we're not too smart."

Life moved with the ebb and flow of the tide, the changing seasons, the crashing sea and the rhythms of migrating animals. The people saw themselves as the direct descendants of animals: bears, otters, ravens, wolves and whales. The animals gave themselves to the hunter only when he showed the proper respect and offered gifts and thanks to the creature's spirit.

Totems tell the stories of the Northwest Coast people. They tell of their family's past, their position in society, their proud accomplishments. Poles have never been worshiped but are instead a monument to the fact that the people and their stories have survived.

Lily followed Frances down the trail. The angry chatter of a red squirrel startled her and she tripped, stumbling, tumbling down a small hill. The thick ground cover cushioned her fall but for a moment she lay still, crumpled in a heap, her hair tangled with moss, her head throbbing.

Dazed, she stared at a dim figure carved in the base of a tree only inches from her nose. She stretched out her hand and traced the rough wood with her fingertips.

"A totem," she whispered as she peered into a large hole at the base of the tree.

Inching forward into moist darkness, she heard the sound of water from deep inside the tree. Suddenly the earth gave way and she fell again, hurtling head first into space.
Down,
    down,
        down.
            "Ooooooh! Ooouch!"

Watchman

Raven

Crouched wolf

Frog

Beaver

Whale

Bear

Raven

Lily landed with a thump. She hugged herself and shivered as an icy fog washed over her. In the dim light she gasped as the swirling mists deepened into the body of a beautiful woman dressed in a whirling gray gown, her hair tipped with silver.

"Who are you?" Lily asked in a shaky voice.

"I am Fog Woman. You are in the First World. You are here to see your world as it was created. Watch."

Spring was gathering time. Long thin grasses were boiled and dried in the sun. Later they were dyed and used to embroider or weave designs in a hat or basket. Many of the traditional designs celebrated details of nature. They had names like "track of the woodworm," "tree shadows," "goose track," or "head of the salmonberry."

Head of the salmonberry

Butterfly

Half the head of the Salmonberry fitting into "the mouthtrack of the woodworm"

Arrow

Wave

ireweed

Teeth of the killer whale

Fern frond

Tracks of geese

There were many sources of dye. Boil grass in salt water, add horsetail
root and the grass turns black; use huckleberries for purple.
For red — "kahn" — soak the grass in an alder bowl filled with urine
and pieces of alder bark. Blue-green or "kheshk" — the color of the
crested jay — comes from adding copper to urine in a hemlock bowl.

A man with a beak-like nose and huge black wings appeared and Fog Woman flowed around him, humming, dancing, making him spin and lift his wings. Lily watched in wonder as Raven divided the night from day, stealing the sun, moon and the stars so Earth could have light, so the trees could grow, the animals hunt, so Raven's people could thrive.

There were four styles of hats. The first was the common 'keep the rain off' type; simply 'root hat' or 'zauk-kaht.'

The second 'big hat' or 'painted hat' was more finely woven and worn by the wealthy.

The third was a ceremonial crest hat — 'shah-dah-kookh.' A very valuable hat with elaborate and exquisite weaving, it was topped with a series of cylinders; each represented a potlatch given by the owner.

The fourth was the shaman's hat. It was only worn when he practiced his magic.

Hood of the Raven

Fog Woman paused by a stream and washed her silvery hair in a basket. As she combed it salmon fell from her comb into the clear water.

"Raven and I were once married," she told Lily. "He thought I was very clever to bring him such riches as these. But he became greedy and began to take my wealth for granted. One day I left him and disappeared into the darkness. He tried to catch me many times but I always slipped through his feathers."

Millions of chinook, chum, coho, pink and sockeye salmon return to the Tongass each year to spawn. Bears, eagles, otters, whales, seals, in fact nearly every critter, in one way or another, depend on the salmon to survive.

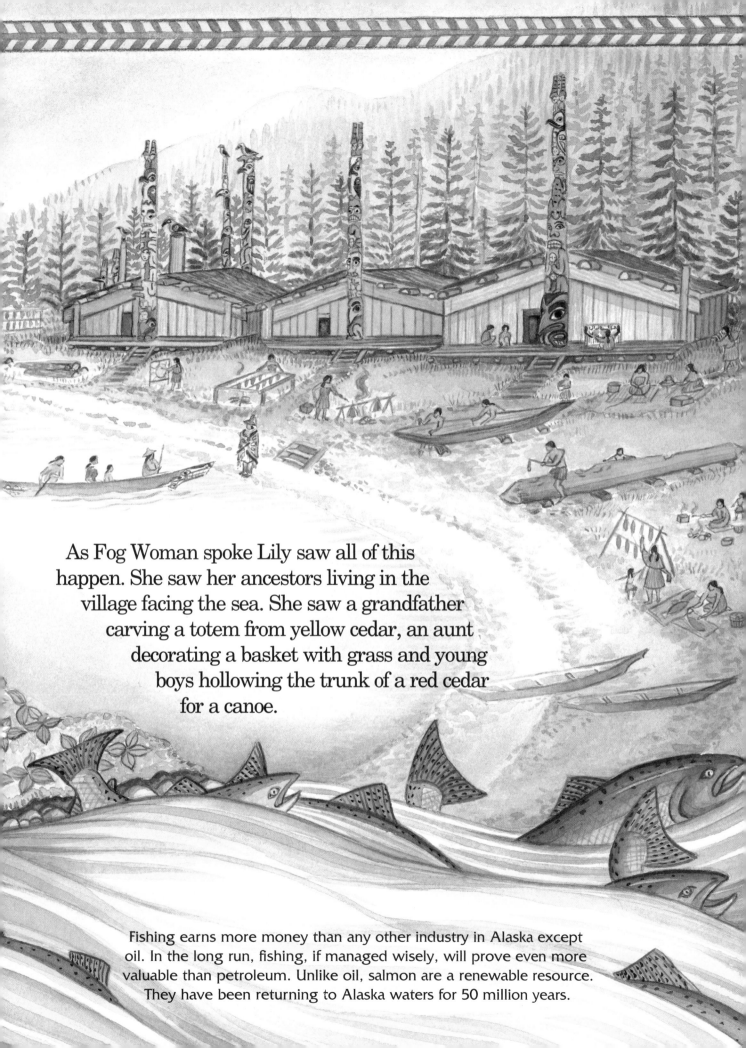

As Fog Woman spoke Lily saw all of this
happen. She saw her ancestors living in the
village facing the sea. She saw a grandfather
carving a totem from yellow cedar, an aunt
decorating a basket with grass and young
boys hollowing the trunk of a red cedar
for a canoe.

Fishing earns more money than any other industry in Alaska except
oil. In the long run, fishing, if managed wisely, will prove even more
valuable than petroleum. Unlike oil, salmon are a renewable resource.
They have been returning to Alaska waters for 50 million years.

Fog grew thicker and the village was gone, replaced by gray slashed earth and an empty sky. The bear and deer were gone. The whisper of water softened the whine of a far-off chainsaw. The only other sound was the harsh cry of raven as he disappeared in the distance.

Lily closed her eyes as she began to spin inside the cloud that was Fog Woman.

"Remember."

Fog Woman's voice was growing faint.

"Remember."

"I will," cried Lily.

Harebells

Chocolate lilies

Forget-me-nots

Salmonberries

Lowbush cranberries

Coastal fleabane

Over the last century clear-cut logging has cut the heart out of America's forests. The practice is seldom used anymore. Only in Alaska, North America's last remaining chunk of wilderness, is clear-cutting widespread. Biologists here report devastating harm to animal habitat. But the profits keep rolling in. The contest is an old one.

The underlying belief that man can control nature and master it for human profit is in many ways in direct conflict with the beliefs of the Northwest Coast people.

Their culture depended on the fish, trees and animals, and they saw themselves as part of the whole, as partners with the wildlife that helped them survive.

Today clear-cut logging is happening on national forest and Indian land. Salmon runs have already been destroyed in the Lower 48 states due to clear-cut logging and dam building. How the Northwest Coast people's lives will change if their trees and salmon are gone is a question they could face in the near future.

Yellow pondlily

Nootka rose

"You will what?" asked Aunty Frances.

Lily opened her eyes and the fog was gone.

"Are you hurt, girl? You tripped and fell down the hill. But look where you landed. This is the tree we've been looking for! The shay-kee!"

Lily studied the tree, a Sitka spruce with bark the color of blood. It's craggy limbs were hung with oldman's beard and Lily could see the edge of a root, thin and supple, anchored beneath a fringe of moss.

"Ha!" Frances cackled, her face split with a grin. "Here are your roots!"

What you can do to help preserve

TONGASS

In Tongass today we have a rare opportunity to experience an intact wilderness ecosystem functioning the same way it has for thousands of years. Imagine marbled murrelets: sea birds that nest in old-growth coniferous forests and prefer to fly inland 50 or more miles each day to nests built from a kind of moss that only appears on trees 150 years old. Many different animals depend on the old-growth of Tongass to survive. It is critical wintering habitat for the black-tailed deer. Standing snags provide homes to woodpeckers, small owls and chickadees. Downed trees stabilize stream beds, providing food for insects, which in turn feed fish like the salmon, Dolly Varden and rainbow trout.

The greatest threats facing Tongass are large-scale clear-cut logging, road building and development. On many federal and privately held lands the trees have been clear-cut across streams and major portions of entire watersheds; a death knell for healthy salmon streams. Fortunately, current logging practices are beginning to change. Clear-cutting is a last resort method in the Lower 48 states.

Perhaps Alaska can learn from others' mistakes. Alaska native corporations and the U.S. Forest Service can adopt the use of uneven-aged management, cutting individual trees of various sizes dispersed throughout the forest. Americans who own these public lands can demand that the intrinsic value of the wilderness be a factor considered as well as other uses and that all alterations of the land depend on sound science and proven management techniques. We can urge lawmakers to stop turning national forest lands over to private interests. These wilderness areas are irreplaceable and extremely valuable — as wilderness. We can have one last, best place in America that stays wild. By educating ourselves we can make wise choices about how we use our forests. Big, beautiful timber can be used to make a Stradivarius violin rather than a pile of pulp. This book is printed on a tree-free paper made of a bamboo fiber grown on family-owned farms. It is a bit more expensive than paper made from trees but it doesn't have to be. Convince local phone companies and newspapers to begin printing on tree-free paper and the cost of producing it will come down! Pronto!

Encourage recycling of paper in school, at home and in businesses. Make sure the paper you use is a recycled brand, then use both sides. Then recycle it!

Don't buy little cardboard juice drinks, paper napkins, small boxes of detergent. Economize — buy the HUGE boxes of detergent and ENORMOUS cans of juice. Carry a reusable cup or mug and reduce your personal use of paper products. Plant a tree. Imagine vacant lots in cities across this land covered with white pine, cypress and sequoia. Call the National Arbor Day Foundation for more information (1-888-448-7337) or the Society of Famous and Historic Trees (1-800-320-8733). Last but not least, call the President (1-202-456-1111), the Secretary of Agriculture, the Secretary of Interior (1-202-208-7351) and the governor of Alaska (1-907-465-3500 or gov.state.ak.us) and the Alaska congressional delegation (202-224-3004 or 202-224-6665) and tell them to stop clear-cutting in Tongass National Forest NOW! Tell them and your local news media why you care about a forest way up in Alaska. Let's save it and someday you'll be able to stand on a silent rocky shore deep in the rainforest and hear the caw of raven as he wings through a rainbow and sails away across the misty purple sky.